When "It" Happens!™ @Work

5 Action Steps to Make Change Work™ for You

Julie M. Smith, Ph.D.

ChangeMatters™

ChangeMatters, LLC

ChangeMatters, LLC
P.O. Box 4252
Morgantown, WV 26504
Phone: 888-9-ATWORK (888-928-9675)

ISBN 978-0-9778208-0-1

Second Edition

10 9 8 7 6 5 4 3 2 1

This book is dedicated to my mom,
Isabelle Mary Bunker Smith

Contents

"It" Happens!™ *is any change that affects you. It can be expected or unexpected, welcome or unwelcome, planned or unplanned, under your control or out of it, caused by nature or by people.*

CHANGE!

A Note from the Author

Regardless of where you work, you will not be spared the depth and breadth of change that is sweeping the world. You name it—economic downturn, mergers, new management, increased job responsibilities, outsourcing, off-shoring, new technologies, organizational restructuring—no industry will be left untouched by change, not even yours.

Today's reality is that organizations must pivot on a dime to execute new business models and deploy new strategies. To survive, *organizations are desperate for employees who can adapt to change.*

This is where the conflict begins. If you are like most people, you crave stability. You want to keep the things you treasure unchanged, from material possessions such as your home, car, and familiar surroundings, to the intangible things such as the friendships you enjoy, the respect you get at work, and the satisfaction of doing a job that you know well. When a change occurs, your "treasures" are threatened.

When you feel threatened by change, it can drain you. At home, it can lead to sleepless nights, family fights, and a general feeling of being out of control. At work, studies show that employees lose two hours of productivity per day when a change occurs. Just when your employer needs you the most, you can't deliver.

This negative spiral does not have to be! You don't have to waste time and emotional energy haphazardly processing a change. This book introduces you to *a proven 5-step process* you can use to become *Change-Resilient—to adapt rapidly to any change with courage and confidence, in a way that makes you proud.*

Watch Gus Makina, the hero of this story, pull himself out of a tailspin when his employer, Heritage Air, is taken over by Upstart Air. As you follow Gus's journey, you will learn a simple but profound process to pull together all the big change pieces—**head, heart, behaviors, consequences to yourself, and your personal impact on others.**

But wait. I bet you are thinking: *Why do I have to do all the work? Isn't my organization responsible for leading the change?*

In the best of all worlds, organizations would know how to deploy change with as little trauma as possible. But even the most change-savvy organizations make lots of mistakes. Change by its very nature is hard to manage—it's messy and unpredictable.

Don't let your personal success depend on the change management skills of the leaders in your organization. Instead, learn to lead yourself through change.

Change-Resilience is a key skill for work and life. When all is said and done, *the quality of your life will be determined not by what happens to you, but by how you handle it when "It" happens.*

Good luck in making *"It"* happen in your life!

Julie M. Smith, Ph.D.

CHAPTER ONE

"It" Happens!™ *@Work*

For twelve years, Gus Makina had been a top mechanic at Heritage Airlines. He knew jet engines better than any man or woman in his shop. He could take one apart and put it back together in the dark, with one hand tied behind his back if he had to. Over those twelve hard years Gus had earned the trust and respect of his colleagues and management.

But now, even though he was a senior mechanic, Gus Makina knew that he'd have to prove himself all over again. His airline was being taken over by Upstart Air. As he stood on the front porch of his house looking down on the town where he had lived all of his life, he thought to himself, *I don't deserve this.*

Gus knew it wasn't going to be a friendly merger. The two companies couldn't be more different. Upstart Air was a cut-rate airline, all coach, no seat assignments, and no meals. Heritage was a grand old lady of the skies, wounded on 9/11.

To compete, Heritage Air had entered the fare wars and cut amenities. Business passengers grumbled about declining service. Fewer flights meant passengers were packed like sardines. And now Gus felt his company would sink even lower by becoming part of Upstart Air.

Gus thought, *I'm not even sure I can make it in the new company— even if I want to. I'm amazed that those crazy Upstart people can even maintain FAA certification to fly. And staying with them would mean having to move across the country to their hub in Philadelphia!*

A few of the men and women who worked with Gus were okay with all the changes that were coming down. It seemed to Gus that they were able to make the decision to stay or to go almost effortlessly, and they moved forward with their plans immediately.

A second group struggled with their decision, but looked forward with hope to the opportunities that the change might bring. Even though they were not quite sure what to do, they trusted that things would eventually work out.

But a third group, like Gus, was stuck. They couldn't believe it—this change was so unfair! They'd done everything that had been asked of them for all those years, and this was their payback? Frightened or angry or worse, they resented this change and the hard decisions it forced them to face.

The longer Gus resisted dealing with the change, the more things began to unravel both at work and at home. After dinner that night, Gus and his wife Joyce started arguing again. This time it was really bad. They both said things they wanted to take back, but they couldn't. So Gus busted out of the house to cool off.

He walked down the long hill from his house to the center of town. In the center of town sat a junk shop. In the junk shop sat an old man. And for whatever reason, Gus walked into the shop that night, perhaps to take his mind off his troubles.

But no matter. Because walking into that store and meeting that old man—whose name was Toskey—changed Gus's life forever.

CHAPTER TWO

Seeking the Key

Outside a weathered storefront hung a sign that read *Toskey the Pack Rat*. On the window beside the front door was taped a yellowing sign that read *Discards Wanted*. After a moment of hesitation, Gus entered the junk shop, a maze of narrow aisles and high shelves that reached to the ceiling. Far in the distance, at the back of the store, burned a dim light.

Gus made his way toward the back, calling, "Anybody home?" When a fat black cat appeared from the shadows, Gus stopped in his tracks. "You open?" Gus called again. But there was only silence. When Gus reached the back of the store, he found an old man sitting at a roll-top desk, working his accounts.

"Excuse me," Gus asked. "Are you open for business?"

"Obviously," the old man replied without looking up.

"Good," Gus said, as he fumbled for a reason to be there. "I'm looking for a . . . a key. See, I bought this antique bookcase. One of the doors won't stay closed. There's a lock but no key. Do you have like a box of old keys I could rummage through?"

Toskey looked up at Gus. He took a good long look, regarding the mechanic from top to toe. Then the old man smiled a knowing grin.

"What's your name?" Toskey asked.

"Gus."

"You may be looking for the key to something, my friend, but it isn't a bookcase," Mr. Toskey replied. Then he swiveled on his desk chair and encouraged Gus to sit.

Gus protested: No, all he needed was a key. But the old man motioned to an overstuffed chair.

"Sit," he said again, and for some reason Gus did. Was it the look in the old man's eye or the kindness of his voice? Whatever it was, Gus sat, and when he did, Toskey said, "What are you *really* looking for?"

There was something about the old man that put Gus at ease and encouraged him to speak. "I guess I'm looking for an answer," Gus said. "I don't know what to do." Gus then laid out his problem. When he finished his tale of the takeover and the difficult decision he faced, he looked imploringly at the junk man. "So, Mr. Toskey, do you have an answer for me? Do you know what I should do?"

The Pack Rat looked at Gus and shook his head sadly. "I'm sorry, Gus. It's not possible for one man to make a choice for another. Even if I did tell you what I thought you should do, you'd just end up having to choose whether to take my advice or not. In the end the choice would still be yours to make."

"So you *can't* help me," Gus replied flatly.

"I didn't say that," Toskey said, as he reached out and dropped something into Gus's hand. "This, I think, is the key you really came looking for."

CHAPTER THREE

The Pack Rat Explains "Change-Resilience™"

Gus stared at a wooden cube in his hand. "What kind of key is this?" he asked.

The old man rocked back in his chair and clasped his hands behind his head. "It's the key to Change-Resilience," Toskey replied.

Gus regarded him dubiously. "Look, Gus," the old man continued, "You probably know from work that people handle change differently. Some react instinctively and just go with it."

"Yeah, that's my buddy Nick," Gus said. "He takes whatever garbage the company piles on us and just goes straight ahead. The way I see it, he's got his head buried in the sand."

"Maybe, but guys like Nick go with their gut, right? And they find it hard to understand why people like you are having a difficult time changing. These **instinctive** people, as I call them, can't describe how they adapt to change—they just do it. And that's the problem: they don't have the words or the tools to help anyone else. They just move on." Gus nodded.

"Now other folks," the old man continued, "are what I call **receptive**. They believe that good things can come from change and are willing to give it a try. But sometimes these receptive folks can get overly optimistic. When things don't go smoothly they get discouraged. As a result, they never completely adapt because they can't turn their good intentions into action."

"That sounds like my wife Joyce—she's definitely receptive," Gus said quietly.

"Now a guy like you, Gus, is what I call **resistant**. Resistant people are negative about the change. They're stuck, unwilling to try new things and move on. But the goal for everybody—whether you are instinctive, receptive, or resistant—is to become **Change-Resilient**."

"But if an instinctive guy, like Nick, just goes with the flow," Gus asked, "why does he have to learn to become resilient?"

"Well," Toskey replied, "two reasons. One, a guy like Nick may run into a change one day that he can't adapt to instinctively. And two, he doesn't have the words or tools to help anybody else. See, to me, *Change-Resilience means that a person can adapt to any change successfully, and that he or she has all the tools necessary to live a productive and self-confident life.*"

"And help other people live that kind of life too."

Toskey nodded. "You may not realize it, but you are a powerful role model for others as you work your way through this change."

Gus thought shamefully of his argument with Joyce and hoped that his son had not overheard.

"When you're Change-Resilient, Gus," the Pack Rat added, "you can handle any change, even a crisis. You can move forward, and by that I mean open yourself up to the opportunities that are inherent in any change, even though you don't see them at first. Gus, you can even improve your overall life for the better, forever, when you become Change-Resilient."

CHAPTER FOUR

The Change Puzzle™

Gus looked at the wooden cube, which had words carved into all six sides. When Gus read the words *My Feelings*, he felt sort of an electric jolt that caused him to drop the cube. When it hit the floor, it broke into six pieces.

"Pick up the pieces," the old man said to Gus, "and put the cube back together. Because, like I said, that Change Puzzle holds the answers you came looking for."

Gus bent over and picked up the six pieces of the puzzle. Each piece said something different:

- *"It" Happens!*
- *My Feelings*
- *My Thoughts & Beliefs*
- *My Behaviors*
- *Consequences to Me*
- *My Impact on Others*

When Gus picked up the *My Feelings* piece, he felt that electric shock again. "What's with this thing?" Gus said angrily, trying to give the old guy back the pieces to his puzzle. "Here, take it."

The old man sat motionless.

"How is a kids' game supposed to help me solve a major problem in my life?"

Still the Pack Rat refused to take back his Change Puzzle. Instead, he told the story of how he had come by the thing.

"About a dozen years ago my wife died," the old man revealed. "I was miserable. Broken-hearted really. I didn't know what to do. All I knew was that everything had changed. But knowing things had changed didn't do me any good. What was I supposed to do with this new life, this life alone?

"Then it hit me. Dealing with change is a lot like putting a puzzle together—only I didn't know what the puzzle looked like. Or even what the pieces were. So I thought about it for a long while and then I carved out those pieces. They capture the areas where I was locked up."

Gus frowned. "What do you mean, *locked up?*"

"I was locked in a cycle of negativity that I couldn't seem to get out of. Even though I felt depressed, I knew I wanted to get back my hope. Those pieces helped me know where to focus my efforts to unlock myself. As I began to work each piece, I started to see the connections."

"What connections?" Gus asked.

"All the pieces are connected. I started with examining *My Thoughts & Beliefs*. Rather than thinking about what I had lost, I thought about how my wife would want me to be happy, rather than miserable. As I focused more on what she would want for me, *My Behaviors* began to change. I knew she wouldn't want me to be lonely, so I started reconnecting with old friends. As I did that, *My Feelings* became more positive. I eventually unlocked all of the pieces of the puzzle."

Gus turned the puzzle pieces over in his hands and questioned how a simple toy could help a man overcome such terrible grief.

"If you learn to unlock each piece and then connect them all," Toskey said, "you'll be able to handle any change that comes your way."

"It can't be that easy," Gus snorted.

"I didn't say it was easy," Toskey said.

The Change Puzzle™ Pieces

1. **"It" Happens!**™ is any change that affects me. It can be expected or unexpected, welcome or unwelcome, planned or unplanned, under my control or out of it, caused by nature or by people.

2. **My Feelings** are the emotions I experience when going through a change.

3. **My Thoughts & Beliefs** are ideas and opinions that run through my head about the change. They are private and known only to me, unless I choose to share them.

4. **My Behaviors** are everything I say or do when I am affected by a change.

5. **Consequences to Me** are things that occur after my behaviors and either encourage or discourage me from doing the same behaviors again.

6. **My Impact on Others** is the effect my behaviors have on others.

(This page describing the Change Puzzle™ pieces is repeated at the end of the book for handy reference)

changemattersatwork.com

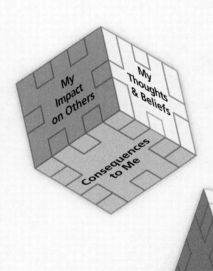

CHAPTER FIVE

Piecing Together the Change Puzzle™

"Remember when you first started working as an airline mechanic and how hard it was, Gus?" the Pack Rat asked.

"Yeah, I remember," Gus said sullenly.

"Is it still that hard today?"

"Of course not. I'm good at my job now, the best in my shop."

"Well, working the Change Puzzle is the same," the old man said. "At first you might find it difficult, but eventually it becomes second nature—that's when you know you're Change-Resilient."

"Okay, show me how to work it then, and I'll work it. Is there some special way it has to go together?"

"Well, there are two important things I can say about putting the Change Puzzle together," the Pack Rat said. "One, always start with the *"It" Happens!* piece—that's your change. And two, you have to put it together in a way that makes sense to you, a way that you're proud of."

"So I put this thing together and then what—is that it? Then I'm Change-Resilient? It sounds ridiculous."

"No, like I said, you have to *work* the puzzle. You can't just slam it together, force in a piece, or leave one out. You can't just say that you don't care whether your *Impact on Others* is positive or negative, for example.

"Gus, there are opportunities in any change. You need to work the Change Puzzle piece-by-piece to find those opportunities.

To do that you have to *think* about how the pieces pertain to your *'It'*—your change."

"The takeover by Upstart," Gus grumbled.

"Exactly," Toskey replied.

"So it goes together one piece at a time. And I start with the *'It' Happens!* piece. I got that, but you said I've got to use all the pieces. You also said I have to be proud about how I put it together. What if I don't want to use one of the pieces? What if using one makes me feel like a schmuck?"

"Which one don't you want to use, Gus?"

"I don't know. *My Feelings*, I guess."

CHAPTER SIX

"My Feelings" Puzzle Piece

"Gus," Toskey continued, "when I first imagined this puzzle, the only thing I knew about change was that it didn't have just one dimension. I knew the change was affecting a number of things in my life. Like my feelings. Which were also having an impact on other people."

"I thought you were alone after your wife died," Gus said.

"I felt alone. But I wasn't," the old man replied. "There were our children, our friends, my colleagues at work—"

"Colleagues in this place?" Gus asked, looking around the empty shop.

It was then that Toskey revealed more of his former life, the one before he opened his weird little shop. He had always been a Pack Rat, collecting one thing or another, musical instruments at first. But back then it was just a hobby.

"My real job was . . . I ran a plant that manufactured plastic automobile parts. But after my wife died, I didn't feel the same about my work. Not proud like I'd been. It was funny, but my feelings about that job that had brought me so much joy and satisfaction, that had meant so much to me and my family, suddenly changed. I couldn't understand why I didn't feel the same about it any more. There were other things I felt different about too. Back then, I was overcome by my emotions."

"I can imagine the grief," Gus said quietly. "It must have been awful."

"You sound like you know about grief," the Pack Rat said, trying to draw out the younger man.

But Gus protested, saying that he hadn't lost anyone close to him, that he had been lucky, blessed even. Both his parents were alive and well. All his siblings and their families were safe and sound.

"But you have a right to grieve," the Pack Rat insisted. "You have suffered a terrible loss too."

"What?" Gus demanded. "What did I lose?"

"With this takeover, you've lost your sense of security, for one thing," the old man said.

Gus felt a rush of emotion. For a moment, he couldn't quite trust himself to speak. He only nodded his head, then finally murmured, "I hadn't thought of that."

Toskey asked Gus if other feelings besides grief were overwhelming him. Gus stared at the old man for a long time before he spoke. "Anger, for sure. Resentment. Apathy." Then the old man watched in sympathy as the names of Gus's feelings flowed like the Mississippi: "Sorrow, helplessness, depression. And fear. Can you feel trapped, is trapped a feeling?" Gus wanted to know. "Because I feel trapped."

"Trapped is a feeling," the old man replied. "Trapped is a terrible feeling."

It was then that Gus broke down. All of his pent-up emotions flowed out in a wild torrent. He started to feel even more emotions. Darker ones: shame, humiliation. He couldn't believe it. Here he was, carrying on like a baby in front of a strange old man. His anger only seemed to deepen.

But when Toskey reached out and touched him, to console him, Gus's anger suddenly abated. "How did you do that?" Gus wondered aloud, feeling calm and relaxed. "Are you a healer or something?"

"It's not me," the old man said. "It's you, Gus. You did it when you named your feelings. If you can *name* your feelings, you *own* them."

"Instead of them owning me," Gus said quietly.

"Yes, exactly. You might think I'm a magician, but I'm not. It's you. You've got the power, everybody does. You and the Change Puzzle. But it's very important to name your feelings to *someone*. A confidant, a friend. Your wife perhaps?"

"Joyce? I've been afraid to," Gus admitted. "And it's funny because Joyce and I used to talk about everything. I don't know why this takeover has had such an impact on me."

"What are you afraid to tell Joyce?" Toskey asked.

Gus hesitated.

"If you can start naming your feelings, Gus, then share those feelings with someone, you will begin to unlock. *Identify and share your feelings*. That's the action step for this piece of the puzzle."

"Okay," Gus said, "sometimes I get—sometimes I just want to tell Joyce . . ." Gus paused. "This is stupid. This is nuts. I don't even know you and here I'm about to tell you like my deepest secrets?"

"What is your deepest secret?" Toskey asked. "The one you're afraid to tell Joyce."

"That I'm scared," Gus said quietly.

Toskey nodded. "What do you fear most about the change?" the old man asked.

"Having to move to Philly, I guess," Gus said. "Hey, it's not that I've got anything against Philadelphia, but my wife and I live in a beautiful house up on Spyglass Hill. It's an old Victorian we restored to its former glory. It's beautiful, Mr. Toskey."

"Your beautiful home . . ." the old man whispered. "Something to treasure."

"Yes, indeed. It is a treasure, a real treasure. And not just for Joyce and me, but for the whole town. We had her put on the National Register.

"Hey," Gus said after a quiet moment, "maybe I'm not so much afraid of Philly as I am of losing the home my wife and I built together."

The Pack Rat nodded. "What other treasures do you have, Gus? Beside your beautiful home?"

My
Feelings

Feelings are the emotions you experience
when going through a change.

ACTION
STEP

Identify and Share My Feelings
To Get Them Out in a Healthy Way

CHAPTER SEVEN

Gus's Many Treasures

As Toskey sat and listened to Gus, he realized that this man, like so many of us, had much to be thankful for. Gus's list of treasures was long. "My wife and son," Gus said without hesitation. "Plus the rest of my family, who live close by, except for my brother Jeff and his family. They live in Wilmington, Delaware, but they all come back home every summer for a couple of weeks and stay with us, since we have so much room. I treasure my books. My paintings—I paint a little.

"Our church, where my son Joe greets newcomers. And Joe's hockey team, which I coach. I get a lot of satisfaction out of teaching the kids to play. And I'm a big sports fan, so I love to take Joe to all the pro games—football, baseball, hockey, you name it."

Then he took a long pause. "And I love my job, Mr. Toskey. I get a lot of satisfaction out of that. I'm an airline mechanic. People's lives are in my hands. I treasure my friendships at work too. And I treasure my lunch breaks every day. It may sound funny, but I laugh more with those guys than with anybody. Except for my wife Joyce, who has the greatest sense of humor. That's the reason I fell in love with her in the first place, I think. She's so smart and funny and beautiful . . . ."

Then Gus grew quiet. He knew he was truly blessed. "I don't want to lose the things I treasure, Mr. Toskey. I don't know what I would do if I did . . . ."

The old man reached out and patted Gus's knee. He nodded his head. "I see why you're so conflicted."

"My feelings are like a cage," Gus replied.

"Those dark feelings that you named are ones that keep you locked," the Pack Rat said. "But there are other feelings that can unlock you."

"What are they, Mr. Toskey? Tell me."

"You've got the answer to that too, my friend, not me. What are some of the other feelings you have about the change? The *positive* ones."

"Well, I'm *grateful* for all the treasures I've got," Gus started slowly. "And I'm *proud* of the job I do. I'm a *determined* guy. That's why I'm so mad at myself."

"Ah, but being mad at yourself is a feeling that keeps you locked up in that cage," Toskey interrupted. "Acknowledge that feeling but don't let it overtake you. Build off of your positive feelings."

"Okay, I'm *empathetic* with my co-workers," Gus continued. "I know what they're going through. I'm *committed* to my family and my community, and to doing good work. And I have to say, I'm a bit *curious* about what the future might bring."

"Excellent," Toskey said. "Those are the kinds of feelings that can move you forward."

The Pack Rat continued, "When you start naming your feelings, you begin to unlock. The trick is to *identify and share your feelings*. The action step for this piece of the puzzle is to understand what you are feeling about the change. Then share those feelings with somebody else. Gus, the one feeling that underlies all locked feelings is fear—fear that we will lose the things we treasure most."

"Like my family, my house . . . my job," Gus said quietly.

"The big thing," Toskey continued, "is to understand and share your feelings. They have got to get out. Sometimes you don't know what the feelings are—that's when you have to take an inventory of yourself, of how you're reacting. Is your stomach tightening? Are you nervous all of a sudden? If you're not sure what's happening to you or why, ask your wife—maybe ask her what signals you're sending. Ask people you trust to help you get at what's inside. Then use those feelings you name—anger or fear—to spur you to positive action.

"Look," the old man continued, "just tonight you've been able to use those negative feelings to move you to another place."

"I don't feel so trapped anymore."

"You're not. You've got one foot out of the cage. One survival tip you learned tonight is to use those positive feelings, like pride—you said pride, right?"

Gus nodded. "But I feel stupid dumping my feelings on you like that."

"It takes a lot of courage to open up. And you've got that too, Gus. Tonight proves it. You've had the courage to share with me. Courage, curiosity, pride—those are the kinds of positive feelings that can move you forward. Another tip is to ask other people how they feel about the change, especially ones who have a more optimistic outlook than you do."

"Joyce," Gus said.

"Good. *Identify and share your feelings*, especially with Joyce," the old man replied. "Now it's getting late, Gus. It's time you headed home. Back to that beautiful house of yours, to your family."

"Wait a minute," Gus interjected. "We can't stop now!"

"You're not going to stop," the old man smiled. "You're going home to talk to Joyce about what you discovered here tonight. It's one thing to talk to someone you just met. It's another to talk with someone you really care about—someone who can help you move ahead, rather than just commiserate with you. That's the next step I want you to take. Talk to your wife. I mean *really* talk to her."

"Identify and share my feelings," Gus mused, as he warmly shook Toskey's hand and headed to the door.

CHAPTER EIGHT

Gus Identifies and Shares His Feelings

It was a brisk winter night as Gus made his way up Spyglass Hill toward home. When he jammed his hands into his pockets to warm them, he felt the pieces of the Pack Rat's Change Puzzle. "Good grief, I walked off with the old guy's doohickey," he muttered, and immediately turned to head back down the hill. But when he got to the shop, it was dark. He peered through the grimy window. The light in the back had been extinguished. Gus rapped on the window, but no one answered.

Questions started to swirl in Gus's head. Where had the old man gone? Would he return in the morning? "Darn it!" he said to himself, his stomach tightening. "You better not be a figment of my imagination, Mr. Pack Rat. I can't do this alone."

Then he stopped and took a brief inventory. *What are you afraid of now, Gus? That the old guy is some spirit who's vanished into the night? How whacked is that? And you are not alone, pal. There's family and friends, all your treasures.* Gus smiled to himself as he headed home. But he vowed to return the next evening, just to make sure the Pack Rat was real.

When he got home, Joyce was reading on the couch, and Joe had gone to bed.

Joyce didn't look up when Gus entered the living room. "It's about time. Where have you been all evening?"

"Talking with a guy." Gus crossed the room and sat down beside her. "I'm sorry for being such a knucklehead," he said.

Joyce put her book down and studied him for a moment. "Apology accepted." She replied. "I guess I wasn't too sweet myself. But please, let's not get into it again. So, who were you talking to?"

"Well, I ran into a guy who has a junk shop in town. We had a long talk about my job."

"You talked with a junk dealer about your job?"

"He's quite the philosopher. He really made me think. He showed me the key to helping us figure out what to do. Whether I should stay with Upstart Air and move to Philadelphia, or stay here and strike out on my own. Look."

Gus handed her the pieces of the Change Puzzle. She turned them over in her hands. "What is it?" she asked.

He began falteringly, "You know how I don't like emotional, soap opera stuff. But this guy actually got me to open up about how I feel about my job, moving, yanking you and Joe out of here, and my fears about hunting for another job. I can't believe I talked to him that much!"

Joyce looked hurt. "Why can't you talk with me about those things? I'm your wife!"

Gus's stomach tightened. *Oh boy, here we go.*

Then he did something he couldn't believe. He turned to her and took her hands. He had not done this since he proposed to her, fifteen years ago.

"Joyce, I'm no good at this, but let me try to talk. I have been so torn up inside about this stupid merger and what it could do to our family. I can't stand to lose our lives here, plus I don't trust the bozos who run Upstart Air. But on the other hand, all I know is how to fix aircraft engines. What other work could I find?"

Joyce squeezed his hands. "I know you've felt this way for a while," she said. "But you've kept it all bottled up and wouldn't talk about it.

I'm here for you through thick and thin." Then Joyce smiled. "Even through richer or poorer."

That broke the tension, and Gus laughed. He talked about his feelings—the good, the bad, and the ugly. As Joyce studied her husband's face, she could see that he had changed. For the first time in a long time, she saw the Gus she had fallen in love with, the determined guy who could be excited about life again.

"This Pack Rat is someone I'd like to meet," Joyce said.

Then they talked about the house and the possibility of moving if he stayed with Upstart Air. Joyce admitted her fears, too. She'd have to find a nursing job if they moved. And she worried about her mom, who now lived alone since Joyce's father died. "If we move, I'd want to take Mom with us," Joyce said. "I don't know if she'd live with us or find an apartment nearby, but I wouldn't feel good about moving if I had to leave her behind."

Gus reassured her. "Of course we'll take Mom with us—do you think she'll want to go?"

"I'm sure of it. I'll talk to her about the possibility tomorrow when I pick up Joe from her house," Joyce said.

"Okay," said Gus.

"I am sure everything will work out fine, Gus," Joyce said.

Joyce's optimism was reassuring, but he was worried that she did not realize the magnitude of what might happen. And he was worried that Joyce would not follow through with her plan to talk to her mother. "And what about our house—you love it more than I do?" asked Gus.

"Yes, I love this old house. But I love you more, Gus. Where you go, I go. I'm sure they're always looking for nurses in Philadelphia." Then she kissed him. And as Gus kissed her, he experienced a feeling he hadn't enjoyed in a long time: peace.

CHAPTER NINE

A Setback

Despite the peace he felt the night before, the next workday proved to be a mixed bag for Gus. He was buoyant throughout the morning as he inventoried his feelings. But late in the afternoon a memo came down, finally proving that all the rumors were true: the maintenance workforce would be cut by 40 percent.

Upstart Air was offering a buyout to middle and upper management. Gus's boss said he was taking the package and bailing out. At the end of the day, as Gus walked to the parking lot with his buddy Nick, he raged at how unfair it was that management "gets a buyout, while all we workers get is the ax and 12 weeks of severance pay."

Nick, a rather practical fellow, noted that Gus had passed up a few chances to be in management over the years. And, he observed that not all the workers were getting laid off. He added that life wasn't fair, and it was pretty foolish to expect it to be. But all Gus could do was vent. "I was doing so well this morning," he said. "I thought I'd turned the corner. Now this! I'm toast and I know it."

Nick, who operated on instinct in times like these, replied, "You're only toast if you throw yourself on the fire, pal." Then Nick slapped Gus on the shoulder and climbed into his car. "Why don't you just go see that Toskey guy tonight? See what he has to say?"

"Forget that. I think that guy's trying to set me up for something. Some scam."

As Nick drove away, he called out, "That's paranoid, Gus! Now you're thinkin' crazy!"

After a quiet dinner, Gus did the dishes with his son, Joe. Joyce watched them out of the corner of her eye as she paid the bills. "Are you going to go down to Mr. Toskey's tonight, Gus?" she asked.

"He's not there," Gus replied.

"How do you know?" she asked.

"I just know," he said tightly. "Believe me I know. Joe, is that how I taught you to load the dishwasher? Look carefully! If you're gonna load the dishes, load them right. Somebody's going to get hurt with that knife sticking out like that!"

The boy looked up at his father with wide, frightened eyes. What had he done to make his father so angry all of sudden? "I'm sorry," was all the boy could manage to say.

"Gus," Joyce said after a long silence, "Joe's got homework to do." When their son had left the room, Joyce looked at Gus, who hung his head, shaking it sadly. "What are you feeling right now?" she asked.

"We got a memo today," he replied. "They're cutting 40 percent of the maintenance workforce. I don't think we'll have to decide on Philly. Heck, maybe it's a blessing in disguise."

But Joyce just grew more resolute. "But what are you *feeling* right now?" she asked again.

Gus stood silent for a long moment. "I feel powerless . . . hopeless." After another silence he said, "I guess I'm gonna go down to see if the Pack Rat's in after all."

CHAPTER TEN

"My Thoughts & Beliefs" Puzzle Piece

Gus breathed a sigh of relief when he found Mr. Toskey in his junk shop. But at the same time, he felt suspicious, even as his new friend greeted him warmly. Why was Toskey so friendly? After some coaxing on the Pack Rat's part, Gus began to relate the events of the day.

Suddenly, Gus stopped to ask the question that was bothering him: "Why are you doing this? Why are you helping me? What's in it for you?"

"What do you think could be in it for me?" Toskey asked.

"I don't know. If you're trying to run some scam on me, I'm not falling for it."

"Is that what you think? That I'm running a scam? Well, I suppose I could be. It's not out of the realm of possibility. May I have my Change Puzzle back, please?"

"What? You want it back? Hey, I didn't steal it or anything," Gus protested. "I tried to bring it back last night but you left." Then Gus handed Toskey the pieces of his Change Puzzle.

The Pack Rat put the puzzle on his desk, then he reached into a drawer and pulled out the new one he had carved for Gus. "This is yours," he said. "After you left last night, I headed home to my workshop to make you one. Here, take it as a gift from me to you."

Embarrassed, Gus took the puzzle and smiled sheepishly at the old man.

"Tonight we talk about *Thoughts & Beliefs,"* Toskey said. *Thoughts are the ideas that run through your head.* They help you make sense of the world, Gus. And *beliefs are opinions that you hold deep-down inside as absolute truths.*

"Let's look at your thought about my trying to scam you. What's at the heart of that? Is it your belief that nothing good can come from the situation you're in—your belief that no one can help you? If nothing good can come and if no one will help you, that leaves only *bad*. Hence, your suspicious about a scam."

"So are you saying that if I believed that positive things could come from this takeover, I wouldn't be so suspicious? Okay, maybe that's so," Gus conceded, "but—"

"And maybe," the Pack Rat interrupted, "if you believe that positive things could come from this merger, you'd believe that *other* people want to help you too, not just me."

"But I still don't get why *you're* helping me. Nobody does anything unless he gets *something* out of it too."

"So the question is what could I get, besides money?" the old man asked.

"I don't know," Gus replied.

"Sure you do. Think."

"Well . . . you're down here all by yourself. Your wife passed away. Your kids could be spread out all over the country. Maybe you need somebody to talk to."

"Very good. What else?"

"I don't know. You went to all the trouble to make me a puzzle. Maybe you believe in this Change Puzzle stuff so much that you want to share it with others."

"Excellent."

"Or, you could—I don't know—be like a guardian angel or something, who's been sent down here to help knuckleheads like me," he added with a laugh.

"That's a little over the top, Gus," the old man replied, "but at least it's positive. Positive thoughts are essential."

"But why are you really?" Gus asked. "Why are you helping me?"

"All the reasons you mentioned—except the angel part, of course." This time they both laughed.

"But you left out the most important reason: I see myself in you, as a younger man," Toskey said. "So what do you think now, about whether or not I'm scamming you?"

"It was a dumb idea," Gus admitted. "Paranoid, like my buddy Nick said."

"You just took a big step, Gus. You challenged a thought and you changed it. Maybe you haven't changed your fundamental beliefs yet, but you changed a thought. That's the next piece of the puzzle. Figure out what *Thoughts & Beliefs* are holding you back, keeping you locked up. And then work through them, one by one."

"How do I work through them?"

"For this piece of the puzzle, *reframe your negative thoughts.* So that negative thoughts become positive. Negative beliefs too."

It was starting to make some sense, how the Change Puzzle worked. Continuing to put his new Change Puzzle together, Gus connected his *My Feelings* piece to the *"It" Happens!* piece—"My 'It' is the takeover," he said, "and I got scared because I feared losing all my treasures."

Then he connected his *My Thoughts & Beliefs* piece to *My Feelings*. "My fears started making me believe that I was powerless in the face of the change. Fear even made me paranoid about you!" Gus could see it was all connected. And he realized that, if he could change his thinking about the change, he could change the feelings that were coming automatically.

"Well done, Gus," the Pack Rat said with a wink, "You're a natural."

When Gus got home, Joyce was waiting for him. She was eager to hear the lesson Toskey had taught him that night. Gus shared what he had learned. He was excited to discover that, the more he talked with Joyce, the more sense the puzzle made to him.

My Thoughts & Beliefs

Thoughts & Beliefs are ideas and opinions that run through your head about the change. They are private and known only to you, unless you choose to share them.

ACTION STEP

Reframe My Negative Thoughts
To Focus on the Positives

CHAPTER ELEVEN

Gus Reframes His Negative Thoughts

Gus spent the next couple of weeks—both at home and at work—trying to think positively, even in the face of impending job cuts that could include him or his friends. When he had negative thoughts and the negative feelings that came with them, he consciously tried not to act on them or amplify them. He found they passed by quickly.

Some days were more difficult because so many of his co-workers were reacting erratically to the merger. They gossiped about their boss: once he'd announced his decision to take the buy-out offer, he had been immediately replaced with a new manager from Upstart named Leona Parsons.

At first, it appeared that she was going to let things operate the same way they always had. Gus certainly hoped that would be the case, because he had the complete trust of his former manager. For example, if Gus believed there could be a safety issue because a part didn't meet tolerances, his manager had backed him up 100 percent.

But less than three weeks into the job, Leona pulled what Gus considered to be a "fast one." She rearranged all of the work crews, and even teamed mechanics from Upstart with those of Heritage.

Gus was teamed with another long-time Heritage employee—Artie Glosser. It was not a match that pleased Gus, but at least it wasn't a guy from Upstart.

After dinner one night, Gus headed straight down to the Pack Rat's shop. He found Toskey sitting at his desk, stroking his fat black cat.

At the outset of their conversation, Gus admitted he had tried to think positively, but events of the past several days kept crowding in, confusing and derailing him. "How can I think positive when everybody's acting crazy, and a new boss throws a wrench into the works? She barely knows our names or what we do, and she changes all the crews. She split up Nick and me—and we've been on the same work crew for six years!"

"What did Nick do?" Toskey asked.

"He just smiled and said I'll see you at lunch," Gus said, shaking his head. "He just takes it. Whatever they dish out."

"He goes with the flow, yes?"

Gus nodded.

"Remember, Nick is instinctive," Toskey explained. "You're resistant, Gus. For a guy like you, it's difficult to think positively in stressful situations. But you can do it if you *reframe your negative thoughts*. Remember?"

"I remember," Gus said.

"It's your action step for this piece of the puzzle. What it means is . . . you turn your negative thoughts around into positive ones."

"You told me that the last time I saw you," Gus replied. "But it didn't work."

"You have to be systematic, Gus. Some folks, like your buddy Nick, don't have to work at being positive. They just are. But guys like you need more help."

Toskey explained exactly how Gus could reframe negative thoughts into positive ones. "When you catch yourself thinking negatively, practice *positive self-talk*. Take, for example, the crew change.

"What could you have said to yourself that would have helped you to stay positive?"

"Beats me," Gus replied. Toskey shot Gus the same look that his father had given him whenever he said "I can't" as a kid.

"Okay," Gus said, "I could say, 'Hey, I haven't worked with Artie Glosser before; maybe that loudmouth can teach me a few new tricks.'"

"That's good," Toskey replied, "except for the 'loudmouth' part. But that's the general idea. Try again."

Gus smiled sheepishly, "How about this: I haven't worked with Artie yet. Maybe he can teach me a few tricks."

"Much better. Always talk positively to yourself. Another way to reframe is to track how many times you catch yourself thinking negatively. Track your negative thoughts, until you reduce their number significantly. Day by day.

"By the way, why do you believe your new manager changed the makeup of your work crew anyway?" Toskey queried.

"Heck, like all managers, she wants to let us know who's boss," Gus replied.

"Do me a favor," the old man said. "When you go into work tomorrow, ask Ms. Parsons why she changed the assignments, just to see if your belief is correct."

Gus looked at the old man like he was nuts.

Toskey smiled. "How are you ever going to know if what you believe is true or false, if you don't test it? Gus, the most powerful way to reframe your thoughts and beliefs is to test them. And when you ask her tomorrow, ask her because you really want to know the truth, not because you want to prove yourself right."

"Okay." Gus agreed. "I am curious to know."

"That's the ticket," Toskey replied. "Now, I want you to take a moment and look into the future. See what your life might look like if you successfully negotiate this change. Go ahead. What would a positive future look like?"

Gus closed his eyes as he imagined a bright future. A small smile appeared on his face. The Pack Rat smiled too. "What do you see?" Toskey asked quietly.

"Me finishing my degree. All I need is nine more credits. Then I see myself in Leona Parsons's job. I see myself managing the dayshift airline mechanics—the people I work with right now."

"Good! That's another tip for reframing: consciously envision what the future might look like if you're successful at handling the change. You can think bigger-picture too, Gus, and imagine yourself, not so much in a specific job, but with a lifetime of employability."

"What do you mean?" Gus asked.

"I'm sure you have many more talents beside being a jet mechanic. You'll start to see more career options when you appreciate all the areas in which you are competent."

"But I am a mechanic," Gus said matter-of-factly. "I've never done anything else."

"Well, don't airline mechanics have to be fast learners because of all the new technology? Don't you have to be a take-charge problem-solver? Don't you have to work well under pressure, knowing that people's lives are in your hands? You could put all three of those skills to use in any number of jobs—ones you haven't even considered yet."

Toskey slowly stood up. "Gus, I'm feeling quite tired tonight. How about we call it a day?" Gus, seeing that the Pack Rat looked a bit pale, left for home.

CHAPTER TWELVE

A Breakthrough with the New Boss

It was late the next day when Gus finally asked Leona Parsons why she had changed the makeup of the work crews. Her answer stunned him.

"Why I rearranged the work crews? Good question, Gus," Leona said. "Maybe I should have told you all the reason when I did it. My people at Upstart are used to my style, but for the folks who don't know me, it's new. It might have looked like I did it on a whim, but I actually did quite a bit of planning and skill-matching to get the right teams.

"See, I wanted everybody to focus. People's lives are in our hands. I was worried that if you were in your old crews, you all might just go on autopilot, since there was so much craziness happening. I didn't want any mistakes. So when I put you in new crews, I figured you'd have to really concentrate on what you were doing. Did it work?"

"Well," Gus said, "we did have to concentrate, that's for sure. Artie and I had to adjust to how we each did things. We had to talk a lot. When I think about it, we did a darn good job, even though—or maybe because—we weren't used to working together. As a matter of fact, I even learned a few things from him."

"You fared better than some of your co-workers, Gus. You got teamed up with someone you knew. Others got teamed with mechanics from Upstart. I'm sure you can imagine how they viewed that change."

"I've heard," Gus responded with a chuckle.

"You'll be happy to know that next month, we'll go back to the old crews. I'll distribute a memo to that effect tomorrow."

"Great," said Gus.

In the parking lot, Gus met his pal Nick. Gus told Nick about his conversation with Leona. Nick admitted his frustration for the first time. "Good. I'll be glad when things get back to normal," Nick said when he heard the news. "I've been working with Doug Spitz, a guy from Upstart. He can't keep up. When I told him he wasn't carrying his weight, he went ballistic. Sheesh!"

"Even Artie and I had to take our time," Gus replied. "It works that way sometimes, Nick."

"Yeah, but it's not efficient—you know that. I don't see why everybody has to make this merger more complicated than it is. I'm outta here!" Nick hopped in his car and roared off, leaving Gus a bit taken aback.

Then Gus remembered what the Pack Rat had said about instinctive guys like Nick, who might finally run into a situation that frustrates them. It sounded like Nick did not have the tools to deal with this change, just like Toskey said would happen. He realized that his thoughts and beliefs about Nick were also changing.

CHAPTER THIRTEEN

"My Behaviors" Puzzle Piece

When he got to the Pack Rat's that night, Gus recounted the events of the day. When he told the story about Nick driving the Upstart mechanic nuts, the old man said, "That's an interesting observation, Gus. It's always easier to see harmful behaviors in others than it is to see them in ourselves. But I'm interested in *your* behaviors."

"My behavior? What about it?"

"What about *them*, not it," the old man replied. "Gus, behaviors are things we say and do when we are affected by change. I want to take some time tonight to work the *My Behaviors* piece of the puzzle. Just like *My Feelings* and *My Thoughts & Beliefs*, there are behaviors that keep you locked up, and behaviors that unlock you."

"So I can get another foot out of the cage?" Gus asked.

"Exactly," the Pack Rat said. "Can you tell me how you've been reacting to news of the takeover?"

"Well, you know how—I've been angry and frightened, and some of my thoughts have been way off base."

"But those are feelings and thoughts," observed Toskey. "Let's switch to your *behaviors*—what others see you do and say."

Gus pondered that thought for a moment. "Well, I'm not much for spreading rumors, like Artie. He's a rumor mill, that guy. And he's been in high gear ever since the word came down. But I can say

I've been acting erratically. It's hard to concentrate. I haven't been able to put together any sort of plan. I don't know—it's like all I can do these days is just enough to get by. I complain a lot, and I didn't used to."

"Good observations," said Toskey.

"And at lunch," continued Gus, "some of us get together and make fun of the ones who are happy about the takeover. I even kid Nick every once in a while for seeming to be so oblivious to what's going on.

"The big thing is, though, I make up my mind to do something—like call a real estate agent to learn what it'll take to put our house on the market—but I never follow through. Yeah, that's a big one for me. No follow-through."

Toskey replied, "It's easy to get sucked into the day-to-day behaviors that keep you stuck. One survival tip is to figure out what you want over the long term, like getting a good price for your house if you do decide to move. Then make a plan and break it down into achievable goals. Plus, as you did today with Ms. Parsons, ask questions to get an accurate read on what you're really up against."

"I need to find out which mechanics they plan to keep," Gus suggested.

"Yes, you do, in order to understand the odds of your staying with Upstart—if that's what you want to do."

"If they're keeping 60 percent of us, that means I could be let go," Gus said quietly. "But I tell you, Mr. Toskey, after what happened today, after talking to Leona, I'm going to ask a lot more questions."

"That's one of the most important behaviors that can help you unlock, Gus," the old man said. "Asking questions brings you knowledge, and knowledge is power."

"I think I'm finally learning that," Gus confessed.

Toskey continued. "But there's more to it than asking questions and gaining knowledge. Based on your new knowledge, you have to come up with a plan with serious action steps. Then follow through on that plan."

"You know that I'll have more questions about that."

"I'm sure you will. But I'll be closed tomorrow night. So I'll see you Monday, if you want to stop by. Now go home and talk to Joyce. Ask each other some important questions. Identify behaviors you want to change. Remember, for the *My Behaviors* piece of the puzzle, the action step is to *make a plan and follow through.*"

My
Behaviors

Behaviors are everything you say and do when you are affected by a change.

ACTION STEP

Make a Plan and Follow Through
Until My New Behaviors Become Habit

CHAPTER FOURTEEN

Gus and Joyce Make a Plan and Follow Through

Friday was an interesting day at work for Gus. He kept identifying behaviors that were locking his co-workers, and trying to change the ones that were locking him. Artie Glosser was truly in high gear, spreading rumors about who was staying and who was going.

Before lunch, Gus decided he had to ask Artie to stop gossiping so much. "I don't like it Artie, when you keep guessing about who's staying and who's going. It gets everybody stirred up and we don't need it. I know you're frightened about what's ahead of us, but—"

"I'm not frightened of anything," Artie interrupted.

"Then you're a better man that I am," Gus retorted. "I've been scared witless and I'm not afraid to admit it. Look, I've been talking to this guy who says that fear is the most common emotion when change happens. And from where I sit, your fear is causing you to spread rumors. You don't have any facts. They haven't even told us how they're going to decide who stays and who goes."

"They won't tell us," Artie replied curtly. "There's no way to find out."

"You don't know that for sure," Gus replied. "We can ask."

At lunch, Gus rapped on Leona Parsons's office door. He asked her point-blank: did she know how Upstart was going to decide which mechanics would stay and which would be laid off? Leona explained there were several criteria: qualifications, experience, work record, safety record, and who's willing to transfer to Philadelphia.

"It's a complicated mix, Gus, but the most important factor is your ability to fit into Upstart's system. Are you willing and able to adapt to new procedures? Those who can adapt have the best chance to stay with the company."

"How am I doing?" Gus asked, grinning broadly.

"Fine, Gus," Leona replied a bit uncomfortably. "But, really, I've only been here a few weeks." Her response disturbed Gus and put him off his game for the rest of the day.

On Saturday morning, Gus and Joyce sat down at the kitchen table to plan. He decided to mentally put aside his disturbing encounter with Leona.

"Let's list things we can do to change our behaviors," Gus said. "Mr. Toskey calls the things we value our 'treasures,' see? And he says that an important question is, *what treasures do we want to get out of this change?*"

"The big question for me," Joyce replied quietly, "is this: which is the more important treasure, this house or your job? Because you can't keep both."

"Is that true?" Gus asked. "Do we know that for sure? If there's one thing I learned from Mr. Toskey, it's that you have to ask questions. You can't assume anything at a time like this."

"Okay," Joyce replied, "but without a job there is no house. I get paid well by the hospital, but without your income, we'd really struggle. We're both key parts of this."

"If we decided to keep this house," Gus said, "that just means I'd be the one who has to get another job."

"You'd be willing to do that?" Joyce asked. "It's not as easy for you as it is for me. Everybody's looking for nurses."

"Sure, I'd be willing. But what if," Gus said, scooting his chair closer to the table, "we said that a beautiful home was a treasure that we wanted for ourselves. What makes us think that we couldn't find one in Philadelphia?"

"But what about family?" said Joyce.

"Jeff lives in Wilmington; it's only thirty-five minutes away."

"Are we moving next to Uncle Jeff?" asked Joe, who had been listening at the kitchen door.

"All I'm saying is that a beautiful home is a treasure for your mom and me. If we did move, pal, all that means is we'd have to find another beautiful home to move into."

"Well, Grandma is one of *my* treasures," Joe announced. "Who would I stay with when I got home from school?"

"Well, your mom and I already decided that if we do move, we'll take Grandma Springer with us," Gus said.

"Cool!" said Joe, joining his parents at the table.

For the next two hours, the family made a list of treasures they wanted from the change. And they created an Action Plan to get them. They set small goals they could really achieve, such as putting aside more money to see them through if Gus were to be laid off, and learning more about the Philadelphia neighborhoods in which they might like to live. That morning, Gus had learned that two important behaviors for him were to talk openly with Joyce and Joe, and to write down his ideas.

That night, Joyce had planned to search the Internet for houses for sale in Philadelphia—the first step on her Action Plan. But she got caught up in a movie on TV and went to bed without completing the task. Gus was upset because he stayed up late to finish the job for her.

When Sunday morning came, Gus was still working, jotting ideas in a notebook. He titled it *My Journey*, and he planned to use it to chronicle his progress during the change. It was only when Joe yelled, "Dad, I'm gonna be late! It's my Sunday to greet new kids at the door!" that Gus put his journal aside and hurried the family off to church.

CHAPTER FIFTEEN

"Consequences to Me" Puzzle Piece

It was a frigid Monday night when Gus returned to the Pack Rat's shop. He heard the old man coughing in the back and found Toskey sitting next to his old coal stove for warmth.

"You don't look so good, Mr. Toskey. Maybe we should postpone this until tomorrow," Gus offered. His wise old friend looked smaller for some reason.

"No," the Pack Rat replied, "I want to talk to you about *consequences* tonight. It's the next piece of the Change Puzzle, and I want to make sure to get to it. You've got to realize that with any change in your behaviors, there are both positive and negative outcomes."

"Well, my behaviors had some positive outcomes this weekend, Mr. Toskey," Gus responded. "I'm keeping a journal, writing down what you teach me and noting behaviors that lock me and unlock me.

"I had a good meeting with Leona Parsons—well, pretty good. I asked her an important question: how Upstart Air would decide who stays and who goes. The one behavior that has helped me most is asking questions—knowledge is power, like you said."

"I'm happy for you, Gus," the old man replied. "Good behaviors result in positive consequences."

"Always?" asked Gus, who then told Mr. Toskey about his disturbing moment with Leona Parson at the end of their conversation. "She looked at me really weird."

"Gus, be careful. You've been flying really high because things have been going your way. But sometimes during a change, positive behaviors—like testing your thoughts and beliefs—can result in negative consequences. You have to expect that."

"I just should've kept my mouth shut," Gus replied. "I blew it."

"On the contrary—you were courageous!" declared the Pack Rat. "Don't give yourself negative feedback for trying new behaviors. Sometimes a new behavior, like asking difficult questions, takes you out of your comfort zone, and you don't like that. Or, you don't get the response you want. But you have to keep trying. Perhaps Ms. Parsons is a bit reluctant to form an opinion about you and other workers until she knows you better."

"I should've thought of that. I'm being stupid."

"No, you're not," the old man replied. "Gus, giving yourself negative feedback keeps you locked too. Staying in your comfort zone keeps you locked. One of the most important things Ms. Parsons did when she came in was to rattle you all out of your comfort zones, by shaking up the work crews. She sounds like an interesting woman."

"She is," Gus replied. "But I can't help feeling that I put myself behind the eight ball with her. I'm afraid she thinks I'm too pushy."

"Stop! Don't let your own negative feedback cause you to avoid your new boss. It's hard work, trying new behaviors."

"Some habits are hard to break . . . like giving myself negative feedback." Gus said. "And look at Joyce's behaviors. She hasn't even gotten to the first step on her action plan. I had to research houses in Philly for her."

"Joyce is receptive and open to trying new things, and now you are, too, Gus. But when you're receptive, you have to stay on task—don't get discouraged when things don't go as you imagined they would. For you and for Joyce to succeed, you'll either need to break down your action plans into even smaller doable steps, or you'll need to work the Consequences to Me puzzle piece. Or perhaps do both," the old man said as he motioned Gus to sit.

"Let me give you the key to working this part of the Puzzle. You can share it with Joyce when you get home. To truly unlock your behaviors, you've got to *find encouragement for the new behaviors you're trying, and avoid discouragement.*"

"Maybe I just ought to stop going in to work then," Gus laughed.

"Your number-one source of encouragement," Toskey said, "is you. That way you don't have to depend on others. Give yourself positive feedback."

"Wait," Gus said, as he opened his journal to write down what Toskey was saying. When the Pack Rat saw the notebook, with *My Journey* written on the front, he smiled warmly and reached over to pat Gus on the back.

"I really moved forward this weekend," Gus continued. "I found this brownstone in Old Town Philly that Joyce thinks is perfect for us. It even has a basement apartment for her mom."

"Joyce is giving you encouragement. That's important. Identify specific people who can support and encourage your new behaviors."

"I was glad to get back to working with Nick today, too. I told him about how I was dealing with my behaviors, and now he wants to get a Change Puzzle too."

"Good. It's about time for Nick, if he's as instinctive as you say, to get involved in this." The old man continued, "Gus, it's essential to associate with people who encourage you. You must not dwell on harmful or discouraging feedback from others. And keep working on your journal. Keep track of things that go right.

"Now here is the last survival tip I'll tell you tonight. If you really want to change your behaviors, try to arrange at least four encouraging consequences for your new behaviors, to counterbalance each discouraging consequence."

Gus noted this new tip in his journal.

"Discouraging things will happen, no matter how hard you try. But the trick is to focus on the long-term positive consequences you want. And in the short-term, reward yourself for behaviors that move you forward." With that, Toskey sat heavily back into his chair.

"Are you feeling tired again, Mr. Toskey?"

"Right now, I'm going through a pretty big change myself, Gus," the old man replied.

"You're not well," Gus said quietly.

"No, I'm not. I'm dying. And it's taking everything I know about my Change Puzzle to work through what's happening to me."

Gus was stunned. "Do your kids know?"

"Not yet. I'm searching for the right time to tell them."

Gus could feel his stomach tightening. He knew he'd have to work his *My Feelings* piece that night to start to make sense of the disturbing news.

Consequences
to Me

Consequences are things that occur
after your behaviors and either encourage
or discourage you from doing
the same behaviors again.

ACTION
STEP

Find Encouragement,
Avoid Discouragement
For My New Behaviors

CHAPTER SIXTEEN

The Nightmare

The news about the Pack Rat's illness sent Gus reeling. He sat at the kitchen table fidgeting with his Change Puzzle, while Joyce sat reading in the living room. She was happy about their working together on the weekend but felt a bit guilty that Gus had stayed up late to discover that Philadelphia boasted some beautiful houses they could afford.

Anger and fear locked Gus again. He felt just as he had felt when he first learned of the Upstart takeover. Could he handle things without the old man, he wondered? Just last Sunday, he had said a special prayer for his new-found friend and "now he's dying!" Gus's faith was suddenly shaken.

But he tried to stay focused, naming his feelings and practicing positive self-talk. "You're proud of how far you've come in just a week," he told himself. "You know what you fear and why. You must use your positive feelings to spur yourself to positive action."

Feeling strengthened, he called Joyce in. He shared the terrible news and the feelings he had kept to himself.

When he told her of Mr. Toskey's illness, Joyce grew morose. "What does this mean?" she asked quietly.

"It means I've got to work my Change Puzzle by myself, and I've got to do it right. What are my thoughts and beliefs about this new change?" he asked nervously.

"Am I supposed to answer that?" Joyce was confused.

"No, I have to do it," Gus replied a bit sharply

"I know you're concerned about Mr. Toskey," she said, trying to reassure him. "You believe that you'll have to deal with this alone. But you won't. I'm right here."

"Yeah, right. Just like you were there for me when I stayed up half the night to search for a house."

"Gus, you're hurt about Toskey," Joyce said softly. "I did let you down the other night, but let's not slip into a negative cycle. We need to support each other now."

"What good is this puzzle stuff anyway if it can't help Mr. Toskey? I can't see any point to it."

"Gus, I'm sure that's not true. Where's your journal? Remember, Mr. Toskey said every change brings hidden opportunities. You could write about the treasures he might hope for you to gain from this tragedy."

"What do I want to get from my friend's death? Now there's a good question! What else can I learn from the old guy? He's given me so much, and what have I given him in return? Nada. Nuthin'. Zip. Zilch."

"Gus, I'm sure that's not true. You're upset. Maybe you should quit for the night. You'll think more clearly in the morning."

"No, I should be able to do this. I can conquer it."

"Yes. But you can't conquer death, sweetheart. No one can."

"I know that! But who says Toskey can't beat this thing. People beat cancer and heart attacks all the time!"

"Gus . . ."

"Forget it, Joyce. Just forget it!"

"I'm just trying to—"

"Joyce, please! Just leave me alone right now!"

Angry and frightened, Joyce headed up to bed. Gus fell asleep on the couch, well after midnight.

That night Gus dreamed an awful dream. He found himself sitting in the board room of Heritage Airlines. Twelve senior executives sat before him in a grim semicircle. The CEO roared, "Now, Mr. Makina, how can you expect this committee to take your recommendations seriously? How can you expect us to believe that your plan to breathe life into this airline is anything other than the musings of a deranged man?"

"My plan?" Gus asked.

"Yes, sir," the CEO replied. "The one in front of you, sir."

Gus looked down at the document on the mahogany table. The title page was typed in bold print and said, MY JOURNEY. When Gus turned the page, he saw that every line read *To Be Completed by Gus Makina*—line after line, paragraph after paragraph, page after page. He frantically looked for the table of contents, the glossary, anything to guide him.

He looked up at the executives. "May I have a moment to confer with counsel?"

"Ten seconds!" the executives replied in unison.

Gus turned and looked. His advisor was Joyce, dressed in her nurse's uniform. As she handed him her stethoscope, she leaned in and whispered, "Listen to your heart, dear."

He turned again and looked into the audience, jammed to the rafters with family and friends. Nick and Artie and Leona Parsons were there. His mom and dad. Joyce's mother. Joe. Gus's brother Jeff. They were all waiting expectantly.

Far in the back of the committee room lay Mr. Toskey on a hospital gurney. He sat up.

"Whoops," the Pack Rat said. "I forgot to tell you one very important thing."

"What is it?" Gus cried. "What is it?"

"Sorry, Gus, no time left. Gotta go." Then the old man floated gently toward the ceiling. As Toskey disappeared through the ceiling, Gus bolted upright on the couch and gasped for air.

CHAPTER SEVENTEEN

"My Impact on Others" Puzzle Piece

The next morning, Gus apologized to Joyce. He busied himself making breakfast for her and Joe, and packed everyone's lunch. She was grateful for his attention, but remained quiet until they put Joe on the school bus and were about to head off to work.

"Gus, I'd like you to introduce me to Mr. Toskey tonight," she said.

"Sure. I should have introduced you a long time ago."

"I'm not sure that's so," she said. Then she gave him a peck on the cheek. "I love you, Gus," she said before walking out the door. "Remember that."

At work, Gus was subdued, bothered by his dream and the idea of losing his friend.

Nick was his usual jovial self again, cracking jokes and chattering about his plan for opening a hotdog shop in his neighborhood. "I've been thinking about it for quite a while now," Nick said. "And this takeover has convinced me that I don't want to work for somebody else, ever again. Gotta be my own boss from now on—"

The thought of losing Nick put Gus into a deeper funk. "What's the matter, pal?" Nick asked. But before Gus could answer, Nick said, "Hand me that wrench, will ya?" Gus handed Nick the wrench and worked quietly beside him. "I'm calling it Nick's Dogs. Short and sweet. Whaddaya think?"

"Sounds great," Gus said quietly. "You love to cook."

"Yeah, but do I wanna cook for a living? There are a lot of issues to work through. I've contacted the bank, looked at a piece of property, even found a griddle on eBay that would fit the space, but—"

Gus interrupted. "You've done all that without even telling me?"

"Hey, well, I didn't think it would be that big of a deal, pal. You know that."

"I'll miss you," said Gus.

"I'll miss you too, bud," Nick said, slapping Gus merrily on the shoulder. They worked together quietly throughout the remainder of the day. As they headed toward their cars, Gus finally spoke. "I really will miss you, Nick. One of the reasons I enjoy this job so much is you."

"Back at ya, partner. But a man's gotta do what a man's gotta do," Nick replied. As he drove away, his glance back at Gus spoke volumes about their long-standing friendship. This was going to be painful for both of them.

Later, after dinner, Joyce and Gus walked down Spyglass Hill to the Pack Rat's shop. Joyce could tell that something else was bothering her husband. It was then that he told her about Nick's plans to quit his job.

The Pack Rat was delighted to meet Joyce. He had made a Change Puzzle for her, too, and presented it tied with a red ribbon.

"I knew Gus would get around to introducing us eventually, but I didn't want to hurry him. He's been going through a rough patch recently."

"I know," Joyce responded. "Believe me, I know."

"Well, our lesson tonight is *My Impact on Others*, so it's only right that you're here, Joyce. I'm sure it's been hard for you, too. Gus has been working very hard to become Change-Resilient. Frankly, I think the reason he's been working so hard are his feelings for you.

"See, unless you're a hermit, your behaviors during a change will have a strong impact on everyone around you—family, friends, co-workers, even strangers like me."

"You're not a stranger anymore, Mr. Toskey," Gus said. "You're a friend."

"Thank you, Gus, that means a lot to me," the old man replied.

"Now, take out your journal," he continued. "The key to working the piece called My Impact on Others is to *check your effect*. That's why I'm so glad you came tonight, Joyce. Gus, check your effect with Joyce: ask her what concerns her most about how you've handled things since the *'It'* happened."

"Okay. What impact have I had on you, Hon? I bet I can list a few things myself."

"Not right now, Gus," Mr. Toskey replied. "Let Joyce talk. That way you can check the effect you've been having."

Joyce started slowly and reluctantly at first. But when she began to share, Gus was surprised by the impact he was having on her.

She said, "Honestly, I've been worried about your ability to handle this, Gus. I'm sorry, but it's true. And I've been embarrassed for you. When you yelled at Joe for loading the dishwasher the wrong way, I wondered what you were teaching him about how to handle change. It's not okay for you to take out your fears on him—you should be his role model. And last night . . . well, you just seemed like you were going to crack. That frightened me. Gus, I can't do this alone. I need you to be strong. I need you to be courageous."

Gus sat quietly for a long time. "Okay. Thanks, Joyce. Really. I need that feedback. And I appreciate it, too. That couldn't have been easy to say."

"Like I said, the man is a natural," Toskey announced to Joyce. "Gus, you're right. It's a great idea to thank people who give you honest feedback. And you did it without my even having to tell you. You listened, even though it was hard. You weren't defensive. Great!"

Toskey continued. "Now tell me about your friend Nick. What effect has his behavior had on you?"

"How'd you know?" Gus asked. "He stunned me today, Mr. Toskey. He just told me he was leaving the company. He'd been planning it for weeks, I guess. He doesn't owe me anything, but—"

"I thought you two were friends."

"Well, we are, but—what I mean is . . . I don't know what I mean. I guess Nick's been going straight ahead, without giving two thoughts about how his behaviors might affect other people. Like me. Like Doug Spitz—he made that poor Upstart mechanic go nuts."

The old man reached out and dropped another Change Puzzle into Gus's hand. "This one is for Nick. Tell him tomorrow to check his effect. Instinctive guys always need to check their effect.

"I know he didn't mean to hurt me when he said he was leaving," said Gus.

"Of course he didn't. He's your friend," Toskey replied. "But when you're in the midst of a change, whoever you are, you have to realize the difference between your *intended* impact on others and your *actual* impact."

"How do you do that?" Joyce asked.

"Gus?" Toskey asked with a serious look.

"You ask them," Gus replied. "You ask them to tell you how your behaviors are affecting them. Like I did with you, Joyce. But you have to be open to what you hear, even if it isn't pretty."

"Now, Joyce, I'd like you to ask Gus how your behaviors have been affecting him."

When she did check her effect, Joyce was surprised and a bit chagrined by Gus's response. "You've been great, Hon. You really have. I'm a very lucky guy and I know it. But sometimes you get like me, overwhelmed, and boom!—no follow-through. Like when you said you'd research houses in Philly on the Internet and you watched TV instead. And you said you were going to ask your mom about moving to Philly . . ."

"And she got really upset when Joe told her that she was going to move with us and she didn't know what he was talking about," admitted Joyce.

"Your homework," the Pack Rat said after a quiet moment, "is to make a list of all the people you care about, and ask yourself whether you are a positive force in their lives or whether you're having a negative impact on them during this time. Then, if your impact is not what you'd like it to be, make plans to change it."

"How about you, Mr. Toskey? I care about you. Am I a positive force in your life?"

"More than you know, Gus."

Before they departed, Joyce asked the Pack Rat to dinner the next evening. "We'd love for you to meet our son Joe, and we'd like you to see the house."

"I'd be delighted," Toskey said.

"What do Pack Rats eat anyway?" Gus grinned.

"Stinky cheese," the old man replied with a wink.

**My
Impact
on Others**

Impact on Others is the effect your
behaviors have on others.

**ACTION
STEP**

Check My Effect
To See If My Impact Matches My Intent

CHAPTER EIGHTEEN

Listen to Your Heart

The next day, Gus gave Nick the Change Puzzle that Toskey had made for him. Gus explained how to unlock each piece, and then how to connect them. But he focused on *My Impact on Others* and guided Nick to check his effect. When Gus explained how the news of the hotdog shop had affected him, Nick became defensive.

"Well, excuse me," Nick said curtly.

"Don't get defensive, Nick," Gus replied gently. "You've got to be open to what people say when you check your effect."

"Okay. Okay. But I gotta say, Gus, it never occurred to me that going out on my own, opening Nick's Dogs, would hurt you in any way."

"It's not that," Gus replied. "I think it's great. It was just your timing. There's been a lot happening. The takeover, learning this Change-Resilience stuff. And the other night my friend told me he's dying."

"Oh. I'm sorry to hear that, pal," Nick replied. "How soon?"

"I don't know. I'm going to ask him tonight, when he comes to dinner."

"You've really taken to the old guy, haven't you, Gus?"

"I have. He's taught me a lot in the short time that I've known him."

That night, Joyce prepared a chicken and made twice-baked potatoes and a broccoli-cheese casserole. "Mr. Toskey will like the cheese, I think," she announced, as Gus stood on the porch awaiting his friend's arrival.

A few minutes later the Pack Rat drove up in a vintage Mercedes 350 SL. When he stepped from the car, Gus was surprised to see that he was dressed in a jacket and tie. No ratty old sweater. No overcoat. No fingerless gloves. He sported a dark blazer and grey wool slacks. His regimental tie indicated an Ivy League university from his distant past.

"Welcome!" Gus called from the porch.

Toskey was carrying a bottle of wine and a cardboard box.

As he approached, he said, "I've always wanted to see inside this house. I've admired it for many years."

After a house tour and dinner, Gus and the Pack Rat retired to Gus's office, an oak-paneled room with a fireplace.

"Very elegant," Toskey noted. "Very commodious. I can see why the house means so much to all of you. Gus, there's one more thing that I want to talk about tonight. It has to do with my own situation."

"I wanted to talk about that too, Mr. Toskey."

"Gus, sometimes, despite your best efforts, you can't unlock all five pieces of the Change Puzzle. When this happens, you have to make a decision about how you'll go forward with the *'It.'*

"When you find yourself in such a situation, you have three choices:

- *you can accept the 'It,'*

- *you can modify 'It,' or*

- *you can create a new 'It.'*

"The only bad choice is to choose to be a victim—choose to stay miserable. For me, that's not an option. So, I chose to accept *'It.'*"

"Your death?" Gus asked quietly.

The old man nodded.

"How soon?" Gus asked.

"Six, maybe eight months. I'll see the spring, possibly the summer. I'd like that. But when you *accept 'It,'* Gus, you must be on the lookout for the hidden opportunities that the change brings about."

"It's hard to imagine opportunities coming from the change you're going through," Gus stated grimly.

"You'd be surprised," Toskey said.

Gus looked at the old man curiously.

"I still have many things to be grateful for. There's you, my friend. And I called my son and daughter today to break the news. They're both coming home this weekend. It will be grand to see them—but, don't get me off track.

"I want to talk about the second choice, how to *modify 'It.'* What you must do is look for ways to alter things about the change, to make it better for you. For example, you might decide to stay with the airline, but look for a position that is more secure.

"Or, the third choice is to *create a new 'It'* altogether, like your buddy Nick did."

"So his hotdog shop is his new *'It.'* I see. Are you telling me this because you don't think I'll be able to unlock all the pieces?" Gus asked.

"No, not at all. I'm telling you this because Upstart will make a decision soon, and you will, too. It could be to stay. It could be to go."

"Stay with Upstart or stay here? Go to Philly or go look for another job? Which do you mean?"

"All of the above," replied the old man. "Remember, Gus, change is multi-dimensional. In any change, you have to accept the things you can't change, change the things you can, and develop the wisdom to know the difference."

Then Toskey opened the cardboard box to reveal its contents—about sixty old keys. "Try these," he said. "See if one of them fits in the lock of your bookcase there."

"Wow!" Gus said. "I forgot. Keys. When I first walked into your shop, that's what I said I'd come looking for. But the truth was, I was looking for the key to Change-Resilience. And, thanks to you, I found it."

"There's one thing I forgot to tell you," Toskey said. Gus felt his heart leap. He reached out and laid a hand on Mr. Toskey's knee for fear that the old man might float through the ceiling and disappear. "What is it?" He leaned in closer to catch every word.

"Don't ever give up!" Toskey said with a smile.

"Change is challenging, but if you listen to your heart and work the 5 Action Steps for each new change, you'll be all right. Make every day count. You can choose to be negative on any given day, or you can choose to be positive. For you, my friend, I prefer positive. I prefer happy."

Suddenly Gus's heart filled with gratitude for having met the Pack Rat. Never had someone so patiently and lovingly taught him such useful life skills.

Gus decided to make this moment count. He reached out to hug the old man, to let him know just how deeply he felt about him.

5 Action Steps

 **Identify and Share My Feelings**
To Get Them Out in a Healthy Way

My Feelings

 Reframe My Negative Thoughts
To Focus on the Positives

My Thoughts & Beliefs

 **Make a Plan and Follow Through**
Until My New Behaviors Become Habit

My Behaviors

 **Find Encouragement, Avoid Discouragement**
For My New Behaviors

Consequences to Me

Check My Effect
To See If My Impact Matches My Intent

My Impact on Others

(This page describing the 5 Action Steps is repeated at the end of the book for handy reference)

changemattersatwork.com

THE FINAL CHAPTER

You Pick the Ending . . .

I offer three possible endings to this story. Why? Because Gus is human, like you and me, and he still has many choices to make. If you were in Gus's shoes, what ending would you want to create for yourself?

Ending #1

Gus and Joyce continued to work the Change Puzzle and complete the plans they had laid out together. They regularly visited the Pack Rat who visited them in return, pleased at the progress his new friends continued to make.

Three months passed. Then the layoffs were announced, and Gus was offered a new position with Upstart Air in Philadelphia. Leona Parsons said that his willingness to adapt to new company policies had been the single most important quality convincing her that he should remain with the company. She was delighted to hear that he was eager to stay with Upstart.

"I thought you might turn us down and open that hotdog shop with Nick," she joked.

"No," Gus replied. "The restaurant business is too risky for me."

"The airline industry is competitive too, Gus," she warned.

"I know, what isn't these days? But the truth is, my wife and I are excited about the move to Philadelphia. I don't know that I'll ever become an Eagles fan, but stranger things have happened to me over the past couple of months."

"We've got an eye on a great house in Old Town Philly, and we're prepared to put our house on the market tomorrow. Leona, I'm eager to see what's coming next, even though I don't know for certain what it will be. Now, that's something I never imagined I'd say! It's funny how things work out when an *'It'* hits."

"An *'It'*?" Leona asked, puzzled.

"A change," Gus said. "A change. You see, the quality of your life is not determined by what happens, but how you handle the change when it occurs. A Pack Rat taught me that."

"A Pack Rat?" she asked in disbelief.

Emile Toskey, the Pack Rat, was better than his word: he lived past the following Christmas. His children were moved by the discovery that their father was so dearly loved by so many people. Gus and Joyce flew from Philadelphia to pay their respects.

At the funeral, Gus stood before the casket, looking down on his friend and mentor. He reached into his pocket, then slipped his hand into the coffin, where he deposited the Pack Rat's Change Puzzle. "Here you go. I don't need this any more. I know it by heart. Thank you," he said quietly, before he turned and headed toward his new life filled with hope and promise.

(If you were in Gus's shoes, would this be the ending
you would want to create for yourself?
Compare it to Ending #2 and #3.)

Ending #2

Gus and Joyce continued to try to work the Change Puzzle, but they struggled to complete the plans they had laid out together. As the Pack Rat's health began to fail, Gus found that working the Change Puzzle on his own was becoming difficult to manage. Day-to-day life got in the way. Joe's hockey team made the playoffs, which consumed much of Gus and Joyce's free time. Even though they had the best of intentions, they never seemed to find the time to follow through with their plans.

Three months passed. When the layoffs were announced, Gus was offered a position with Upstart Air in Philadelphia. But he and Joyce weren't quite prepared for the offer, and it sent them both into a tailspin. Joyce's mother changed her mind about leaving home and moving far from family and friends. Secretly she worried that for all their good intentions, Gus and Joyce's plans wouldn't work out.

Gus and Joyce argued, until they finally agreed that Gus would take an apartment in Philadelphia and Joyce and Joe would follow when the school year ended. Gus visited on weekends, to stay connected with the family he loved. But overtime caused him to miss important weekends. At the end of the school year, Joe announced that he didn't want to move. Gus felt trapped once again.

Emile Toskey reached out to Gus several times but Gus was too far away and too preoccupied to maintain their strong connection. Gus did hurry back when his friend was near death. Standing over his hospital bed, Gus couldn't hold back the tears.

"It's just part of the process, Gus," the old man said.

"I know, Mr. Toskey," Gus replied. "But some parts of the process are too hard."

At the funeral, Gus stood before the casket, looking down on his friend and mentor. He reached into his pocket, and returned the Change Puzzle that the Pack Rat had carved for him. "Thanks for trying, old friend. This works for you, but I don't think it'll ever work for me." After the funeral, Gus headed back to his apartment in Philadelphia, alone.

(If you were in Gus's shoes, would this be the ending
you would want to create for yourself?
Compare it to Ending #1 and #3.)

Ending #3

Gus and Joyce continued to work the Change Puzzle in order to complete the plans they had laid out together. They regularly visited the Pack Rat who visited them in return. He was pleased at the progress his new friends were making.

Three months passed. Then the layoffs were announced, and Gus was not offered a new position with Upstart Air in Philly. Leona Parsons explained that the company had to make deeper job cuts than they originally had announced.

"You've adapted extremely well to your new work environment and culture," she explained. "But, instead of cutting 40%, we had to cut 70%."

Gus was disappointed, but he was prepared.

"Are you going to open the hotdog shop with Nick?" Leona asked.

"No," Gus replied. "Restaurants are too risky for me. And I've met this man who's got a fairly established antiques business. When I first met him, I thought he just ran a junk shop, but he has clientele in New York, Los Angeles, Paris, all over the world. We've talked and he wants to take me on as his partner."

"The antique business is competitive too, Gus," she warned.

"I know," he replied. "What isn't these days? But the truth is, my wife and I like old houses and antiques, and this is an opportunity for me to go off in a new direction, something I never imagined. It's funny how things work out when an *'It'* hits."

"An *'It'*?" Leona asked, puzzled.

"A change," Gus responded. "An *'It'* is a change."

Emile Toskey, the Pack Rat, was better than his word: he lived past the next Christmas. Gus and Joyce were with him when he died, as were his children, who were pleased to know that the business their father loved so much was in good and able hands.

At the funeral, Gus stood before the casket looking down on his mentor and business partner. He reached into his pocket, and gave his friend's Change Puzzle back to him. "Here you go. I've got it," he said quietly. Then he walked out—toward his new life filled with hope and promise.

> *(If you were in Gus's shoes, would this be the ending*
> *you would want to create for yourself?*
> *Compare it to Ending #1 and #2.)*

Book Discussion Guide

1. Gus was surprised at the announcement of his company's merger plan. It caught him off guard. What were some of his initial Thoughts and Feelings?

2. Were you able to relate to his dilemma?

3. How had Mr. Toskey (the Pack Rat) learned to be Change-Resilient?

4. Think about each character in the story, and the 4 Typical Reactions to Change on the facing page. How would you label each character's reaction to change: Resistant, Receptive, Instinctive, or Resilient?

Character	Reaction type	Why did you select this type?
Gus		
Joyce		
Nick		
Mr. Toskey		

4 Typical Reactions to Change

Resistant

- Has mainly negative Feelings and Thoughts & Beliefs about the change
- Shows active or passive resistance
- Is unwilling to try new things to move on

Receptive

- Is emotionally ready for the change and believes opportunities will arise
- Willingly tries new things but becomes easily discouraged
- Unable to turn good intentions into action

Instinctive

- Moves forward instinctively and adapts successfully
- Doesn't have the words or tools to help others adapt
- Might be viewed as insensitive to others struggling through the change

Resilient

- Adapts successfully by working the 5 Action Steps as the change unfolds
- Has the words and tools to help others adapt
- Achieves the best possible outcome for self, others, and the organization

5. How did Gus "Unlock" to become Resilient?

	The 5 Action Steps	How did Gus do it?
My Feelings	*Identify and Share My Feelings*	
My Thoughts & Beliefs	*Reframe My Negative Thoughts*	
My Behaviors	*Make a Plan and Follow Through*	
Consequences to Me	*Find Encouragement, Avoid Discouragement*	
My Impact on Others	*Check My Effect*	

6. Which of the three endings did you prefer? In each ending, what additional changes and challenges do you see for Gus and his family? What kind of ending would you want to create for yourself?

7. What did you like most about this story? Which of the 5 Action Steps will you use now or in the future?

(End of Discussion Guide)

A Change Workshop
for Everyone

*"A very creative approach
to introduce an extremely powerful
change model and easy-to-use tools
that people 'get' immediately."*

–A Satisfied Customer
Used the Change Workshop
to accelerate a merger and restructuring

ChangeMatters™
For Everyone @Work™

A TURN-KEY SOLUTION

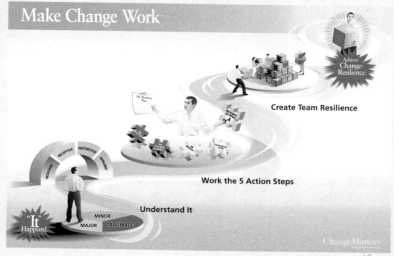

Make Change Work™

Achieve Change-Resilience

Create Team Resilience

Work the 5 Action Steps

Understand It

"It Happens!"

MINOR
MAJOR TRAUMATIC

RESISTING DECEPTIVE INSTINCTIVE ENGAGING

ChangeMatters

Developed with Root Learning **root**

Employees lead themselves on a journey of understanding and aligning:

- Organizational Change
- Personal Change-Resilience
- Dynamic Team Resilience

Highly interactive discussion is guaranteed with the use of the following:

- **Table Map:** *Make Change Work™* Process Visual

- **Content Cards:** Provide a framework and a common language

- **Discussion Guide:** Creates an engaging environment to explore complex change topics

- **Facilitator Guide:** Keeps the conversation on track (no special training needed)

- **DVD:** Communicates key concepts

EASY TO DEPLOY

- Leader-led or supported by HR—no need to be a "change expert"
- Can be cascaded—from senior leaders to frontline
- Audience size—from 5 to 500 (or more!)
- Can be delivered virtually
- Discussion questions can easily be updated, customized, or regionalized
- Easy to use in many ways:
  - Standalone workshop
  - Inserted into existing change leadership workshops
  - Supplement to your organizational change model and tools
  - Front-end of a change deployment

WITH OPTIONAL RESOURCES

- **Book:** When *"It"* Happens!™ @Work: 5 Action Steps to Make Change Work™ for You

- **Personal Action Plan:** A practical tool that helps employees develop their own Change-Resilience Plan (online or in the Change Planner– see page 86)

A Change Planner
for Everyone

*"If you want your organization
to move beyond just talking
about a strategic change and actually
making the change happen,
then use this process."*

–A Satisfied Customer
Used the Change Planner for global
restructuring and outsourcing initiative

ChangeMatters™
For Everyone @Work™

Make Change Work™

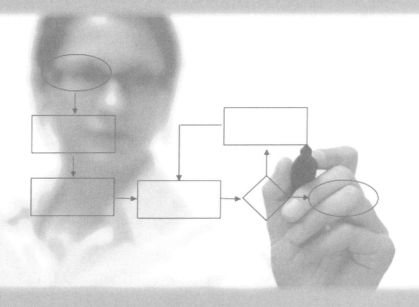

A Change Planner
for Everyone

A powerful, streamlined
process to implement
strategic changes deep
into your organization

For more
information about the
Change Planner,
contact ChangeMatters
at **888-9-ATWORK
(888-928-9675)** or visit
**changematters
atwork.com**

FINALLY—A ONE-PIECE PLANNER TO DEPLOY ANY CHANGE, BIG OR SMALL!

Just like change unfolds, the Planner unfolds just-in-time, to help leaders and employees understand what a change means to them personally, to their teams, and to the organization.

Use it to accelerate adaptation and commitment to *any* change, from local work team changes to larger, global initiatives.

STAGE 1: UNDERSTAND THE ORGANIZATIONAL CHANGE

- Ensure company-wide communication
- Surface and discuss issues
- Help all levels of employees understand what the change means to them
- Get company-wide commitment to make the change work

STAGE 1: ORGANIZATIONAL CHANGE PLAN (UNDERSTAND IT)

CRITICAL INFORMATION FOR ME TO TAKE BACK TO THE JO

THE ORGANIZATIONAL CHANGE IS:

QUESTIONS I HAVE:

Understand It

MINOR
MAJOR TRAUMATIC

"It" Happens!

Part of the Planner

STAGE 2: DEVELOP A PERSONAL CHANGE-RESILIENCE™ PLAN

Help employees personally adapt to your organizational change using our proven **5 Action Steps**:

Identify and Share My Feelings
To Get Them Out in a Healthy Way

Reframe My Negative Thoughts
To Focus on the Positives

Make a Plan and Follow Through
Until My New Behaviors Become Habit

Find Encouragement, Avoid Discouragement
For My New Behaviors

Check My Effect
To See If My Impact Matches My Intent

QUICK SELF-CHECK TOOLS FOR INDIVIDUALS

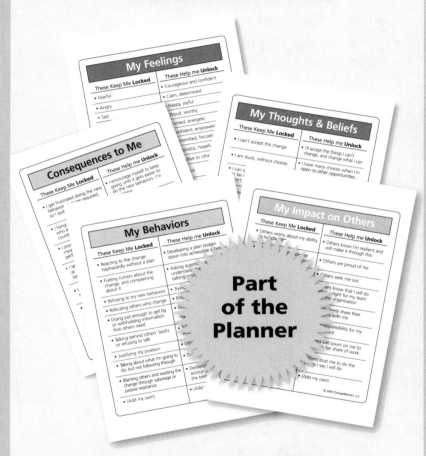

The personal planning section provides employees with proven tools to identify if they are open to a specific change—or resisting it. Specific Actions are included to help employees unlock and move forward in a way that insures success for themselves, others they care about, and the organization.

STAGE 3: CREATE TEAM RESILIENCE

The team works together to:

- Define exactly how the team will be impacted by the change

- Agree on short-term business priorities

- Decide what they'll start, stop, and continue doing to achieve those priorities

- Identify how they will support one another through the change to create dynamic team resilience

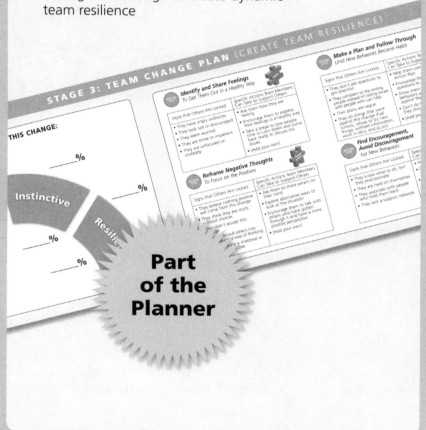

Part of the Planner

SHARE *"IT"* WITH OTHERS

Features a **Discussion Guide** to help employees apply key learnings to their own situation

Quantity discounts are available.

For details on quantity purchases, or to learn more about ChangeMatters products and workshops, call **888-9-ATWORK (888-928-9675)** or visit our website at **changemattersatwork.com**

Acknowledgments

As a veteran change leadership consultant, I have worked closely with people from a variety of jobs, from executives of Fortune 100 companies to front-line employees in local mom-and-pop shops. This book is dedicated to all of those brave souls who confided in me during times of change in their organizations.

I've heard untold stories of how people's lives were adversely affected by even the most minor of organizational changes. I could see that some were resentful of change and full of anger. Others would say they welcomed change, but I'd come back a month later and they would have accomplished nothing. Only a few were resilient, able to adapt quickly and to create success for themselves, their families, and the organization.

I knew that change did not have to involve all this personal trauma and wasted effort. So, I went on a decade-long quest to find the tools to help people to become Change-Resilient. I wanted to develop a process that people could use to lead themselves through change, so they wouldn't have to be helpless victims of the inevitable changes that happen in life—at work, at home, and in the world.

My clients have helped shape these tools to the point where we know they work. My clients have used these tools to help people through a variety of changes including SAP implementations, reorganizations, mergers, job changes, retirements, the outsourcing of jobs, and so on.

I'd like to thank all those people who piloted the tools. You unselfishly shared your stories of how you put them to use, took them home to share with family and friends, and provided feedback on how to improve them. Key people include Heidi Bohlman, Linda Hunley, Linda Alexander, Steve Pendill, Jay Duffy, Kevin Munson, Nelson Frye, Michael McNally, Olivia Meade, George Lamperti,

Robert Coates, Hilary Potts, Marcia Corbett, David Horowitz, Lynn Hillis, and Nancy Urell.

I'd like to offer a special thanks to the team who helped develop this book and the complementary workshops, *Make Change Work*™ and *Leading Others Through Change*. This incredible team includes: Carol Solomon, Amy Avergun, Scott Frank, David Foreman, Fred Schroyer, Amy Fastenau, Art Bauer, Tim Armstrong, Stephanie Glidden, Don Hancock, Roxanne Koepsell, and Joyce Shafer. You worked tirelessly to help make complex ideas simple and accessible. I am forever grateful to all of you.

Finally, thanks to my husband Mickey. You are the most patient person I know. Thanks for the many treasures you bring to my life. I feel rich beyond belief because I am with you.

Julie M. Smith, Ph.D.

Founder and CEO, ChangeMatters, LLC
Cofounder, CLG, Inc.

Julie founded ChangeMatters, LLC, an innovative provider of proven, personal change tools that help individuals enact change in their lives with courage and self-confidence—to truly become Change-Resilient.

Julie has pioneered some of the most powerful and practical change tools available today. As a cofounder of CLG, Inc., a global consulting company, she has helped Fortune 100 companies apply CLG's behavior-based Performance Catalyst for Change℠ methodology to execute strategic initiatives quickly and successfully.

Julie has an impressive track record of helping individuals and organizations face, formulate, and implement change—including Fortune 100 companies. She has achieved major client results with a variety of complex strategy execution efforts, including leading the world's largest outsourcing, jump-starting customer service in a global airline, coaching leaders in a Pan-European turnaround, and improving Return On Capital Expended in a major oil company.

Julie has published numerous articles covering topics such as innovation management, formalized mentor systems, strategic planning models, and quality of work life. She coauthored the book *Performance Analysis: Understanding Behavior in Organizations* and recently launched three books, *"It" Happens!™ How to Become Change-Resilient, When "It" Happens!™ @ Work: 5 Action Steps to Make Change Work™ for You,* and *When "It" Happens!™ to Your Health: 5 Action Steps to Take Control of Your Recovery.™*

Julie spearheaded a grassroots, community-based effort to improve the health of women in West Virginia. Using a holistic, pro-health message of personal empowerment, women throughout the state are given a framework to create healthy lifestyle choices. Beginning with a powerful one-day retreat, women inspire and motivate each other to take the first step, or an extra step, to become healthier. As women carry forward their learnings and supportive relationships from the retreat, they are having a broad impact on their families, friends, and communities.

In her keynote presentations, Julie incorporates extensive experience, humor, and real-world examples from her consulting engagements and one-on-one coaching relationships. Audiences at all levels say that she brings a masterful clarity to even the most complex change issues and leaves them with tools they can put to use immediately.

At West Virginia University, Julie serves on the School of Medicine Visiting Committee and the College of Arts and Sciences Advisory Board. She is as an adjunct faculty member in the Psychology Department.

Julie lives with her husband Mickey in Morgantown, West Virginia, where they enjoy building a riverside park surrounded by their human family and animal friends—five lazy llamas, and one headstrong miniature horse.

The Change Puzzle™ Pieces

1. **"It" Happens!**™ is any change that affects me. It can be expected or unexpected, welcome or unwelcome, planned or unplanned, under my control or out of it, caused by nature or by people.

2. **My Feelings** are the emotions I experience when going through a change.

3. **My Thoughts & Beliefs** are ideas and opinions that run through my head about the change. They are private and known only to me, unless I choose to share them.

4. **My Behaviors** are everything I say or do when I am affected by a change.

5. **Consequences to Me** are things that occur after my behaviors and either encourage or discourage me from doing the same behaviors again.

6. **My Impact on Others** is the effect my behaviors have on others.

changemattersatwork.com

5 Action Steps

Identify and Share My Feelings
To Get Them Out in a Healthy Way

Reframe My Negative Thoughts
To Focus on the Positives

Make a Plan and Follow Through
Until My New Behaviors Become Habit

***Find Encouragement,
Avoid Discouragement***
For My New Behaviors

Check My Effect
To See If My Impact Matches My Intent

changemattersatwork.com